Fiverr Boot Camp

Join the GIG Economy. Make More Money, Enjoy More Freedom.

Table of Contents

Read This First

One way an e-commerce website can tell it's made the big-time is when everyone and their brother writes a book about how to make money using it. If that's the gauge, then Fiverr is an e-commerce colossus.

By my count, there are 37 books for sale on Amazon that explain how to list and sell your services on Fiverr. I read every one of them. Thank God, most of them were short. You can easily tell the ones that were written by non-English speakers. The words are all jumbled up, and out of sync—sort of like watching a movie where the voices don't match up with the people talking. I can't help but think the authors should have ordered a Fiverr translation gig. It would have made reading all those books easier on me, and countless other readers.

Anyway, here comes book number 38. I've done my best to provide the info you need to get started today and grow your Fiverr gigs to be as successful as you want them to be.

Let's get started.

The Very Least You Need to Know

Fiverr is relatively new to the e-commerce scene.

Micha Kaufman and Shai Wininger founded the company in 2010. All gigs start at $5.00, but that's changing as the site continues to reinvent itself. Sellers receive $4.00 for each completed gig. Fiverr's take is twenty percent or $1.00 from each five-dollar gig.

As of October 2016, there were over three million gigs listed on Fiverr. The bad news is over one million of those gigs didn't receive a bite—not one. If that's not a good reason to read this book, I don't know what is.

Fiverr has a leveling system, like eBay's Top-Rated Seller Program.

- **Newbies** have limited options on Fiverr. They can offer two gig extras limited to $5.00, $10.00, and

$20.00. New sellers are limited to accepting four gigs in one transaction.

- **Level One** status opens up more opportunities for sellers. To reach Level One status, Fiverrs need to complete ten gigs in the previous thirty days with a minimum 90% satisfaction rating. After they level up, sellers can list up to 15 gigs at a time, offer "fast delivery" for extra profits, and provide custom orders up to $1500. Level One status also opens up another gig extra—for a total of three, and allows sellers to accept eight orders in one transaction.
- **Level Two Sellers** are required to have completed 50 gigs in the last sixty days with a minimum 90% satisfaction rating. When they reach this level, sellers can increase their income significantly. Buyers can purchase up to twelve of their gigs at one time. Gig Extras jump to five, and the price range increases to $5.00, $10.00, $20.00, and $40,00.
- Becoming a **Top-Rated Seller** is like receiving tenure at a major university. The process for reaching this status is somewhat mysterious. The Fiverr blog states **the site editors "mutually" choose top Rated Sellers**. What is clear though is once you receive this designation a whole new world of profit possibilities open up to you. **Top-rated Sellers** can charge up to $100 for each gig extra, and they receive the **Top-Rated Seller** Badge next to each of their gigs.

If you're serious about making money on Fiverr, you need to level up as quickly as possible. The easiest way to do this is to offer a variety of gigs and provide excellent customer service.

Jon says it took him "a week to move from **Newbie** to **Level One**. In another thirty days, I had my **Level Two** badge. From my very first day on Fiverr, the orders kept pouring in. And, do you want to know why? Because all of my gigs offered great value, people spent their money with me.

"I didn't worry about how much money I was making, or how long it took to do the job. The *Golden Ticket* I was shooting for was *five-star feedback*. Three months after I started on Fiverr, I had a perfect feedback rating on 257 sales.

"That's worth more than any amount of money I could have made at that time. It opened up bigger gig extras, larger dollar sales, and, did I mention—less than two years later, Fiverr selected me as a **Top-Rated Seller**."

Sell it on Fiverr

Fiverr is a freelance hub where buyers and sellers can exchange cash for services. What amazes me is every item featured on Fiverr starts at only $5.00—almost.

There appears to be no limit to the types of services sellers can offer on Fiverr. Among the recent gigs (what Fiverr calls listings) are –

- Custom logo design
- Facebook header design
- Amazon book reviews and product reviews
- Puppet videos
- Kindle and eBook book covers
- Tarot readings
- Psychic readings
- Resume and cover letter writing
- Poetry Writing
- Business card design
- Infographic design

By now hopefully, you get the idea. If you can imagine it, you can find a way to offer it as a gig on Fiverr.

Gig extras, the key to moving beyond $5.00

Earlier I mentioned gig extras.

Gig extras are the method Fiverr has devised to let sellers take their income to the next level. To better understand how gig extras work, check out these extras offered by Professor Puppet.

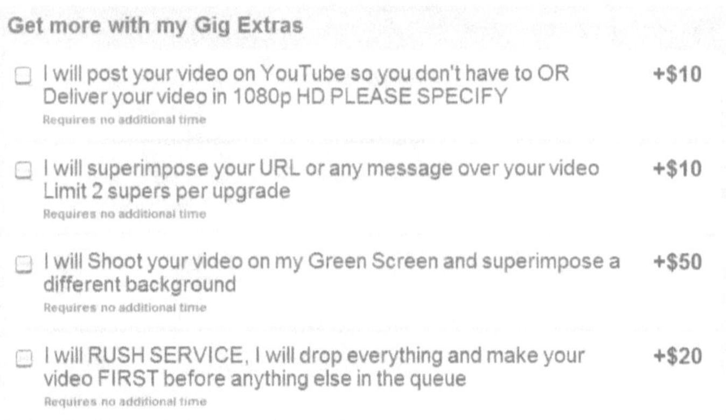

Get more with my Gig Extras

- ☐ I will post your video on YouTube so you don't have to OR Deliver your video in 1080p HD PLEASE SPECIFY — +$10
  Requires no additional time
- ☐ I will superimpose your URL or any message over your video Limit 2 supers per upgrade — +$10
  Requires no additional time
- ☐ I will Shoot your video on my Green Screen and superimpose a different background — +$50
  Requires no additional time
- ☐ I will RUSH SERVICE, I will drop everything and make your video FIRST before anything else in the queue — +$20
  Requires no additional time

Even though every gig on Fiverr starts at $5.00, Professor Puppet can increase his take to $95.00 if someone decides to add all his gig extras to their order.

And, just in case you think most buyers stick with the basic $5.00 offer, think again! Professor Puppet made two promotional videos for my businesses. Each time I spent over $35.00.

So, if anyone out there is still wondering how you can make money selling each of your services for only five bucks, you know the answer – **GIG EXTRAS**. They can quickly raise your average $5.00 sale to $25.00, or more.

One final thought on gig extras. The best gig extras don't necessarily have to cost you more time or money.

Most sellers offer very simple gig extras:

- Next day service for five, or ten dollars
- A PSD file of the graphic they already designed for an additional $5.00 to $20.00. It's no extra work – you already have it on your computer.
- Two more revisions for $5.00, or $10.00.
- Your video delivered in additional formats for $10.00, or $20.00.
- A 3D cover to go with the 2D eBook cover they already designed for an additional $5.00.

The key to making the most money on Fiverr is to keep your gig extras uncomplicated and easy to perform, but still, make them appear valuable to your customers.

Tomasso has been selling on Fiverr for two years now. "I didn't worry about gig extras when I got started," he said. "I was making $2500 a month, five bucks at a time.

"Why complicate things?

"That's what I thought. But, one day I read a story on the Fiverr blog about a guy who doubled his income after he added gig extras to his listings.

"That got my attention.

"He said one out of eight orders gave him an extra ten dollars just for providing next day delivery. It didn't take any more work. He just switched up their place in the queue. He received an extra $25.00 when he charged a commercial use fee for his drawings. Again, it didn't involve any more work. He just emailed the buyer a commercial use release. Now Fiverr offers this as a gig extra, so it's even easier.

"It didn't make any sense to me, but I gave it a shot. And, crazy as it sounds, people started paying me more money.

"All I can say is try it; you'll like it."

I saved the best part for last. After sellers have asked for and collected payment for their gig extras, many sellers dangle a new-fangled cyber tip jar out there that lets them earn even more money.

If you want to make even more money, the key is to give customers a compelling, or downright crazy reason to give you an extra-large tip.

One seller suggests for an additional $5.00; he could start his day with a latte from Starbucks, for $20.00 he could put a half a tank of gas in his old jalopy, and for $50.00 he would have a good start at taking his wife out for a romantic supper.

Who could resist giving this creative genius a tip?

How do you get started?

Getting started as a seller on Fiverr is as easy as entering your email address and choosing a username and password. That's it, and you're a member of the Fiverr community.

Before you click the join button, you need to take a few moments to think about your username. It's how people will come to know you on Fiverr.

A relevant username that complements the service you are providing will help to position you as an expert in the service you are offering.

Many people choose the first idea that pops into their head, or maybe their name. The thing is, if you name your business marysue or wonderwoman 113, people aren't going to have any idea what you do.

If you call yourself videoreviewer or bestlogodesigner, people are going to know right away what services you offer. A professional username can help position you as the best seller for the job.

Seller basics

Every gig on Fiverr starts with the words "I will ___for $5.00." Or, I should say, every gig used to say what they would do for $5.00. Now that Fiverr lets sellers set a higher starting price it says, "I will_____." The title no longer contains a price.

As a seller, your job is to fill in the blank. Just what is it you're willing to do for five bucks?

I know, some of you are saying – not much.

A recent Fiverr survey says there are thousands of sellers making $1000 to $2000, or more, every month. Some of the elite Fiverrs make $5000 or more each, and every month.

So, before you turn your nose up at five bucks, let's examine some of the things you need to consider before creating your first gig.

Before you do anything, check out the Fiverr website for two or three days. Explore the different categories, and click into as many gigs as you can.

Keep your pen and notebook handy. Whenever you see something you like or a gig you might want to do – jot it down.

Write down the seller's username – the title of their gig – keywords they use to describe their gig – any special instructions they include in their descriptions. It's valuable information you can use later to help craft your gigs.

Don't stop there. Check out any pictures, or samples they include. If the seller has a video describing the service they are offering, watch it, and make a few notes about what they say, and how they describe their gig.

Read the feedback left for some of the gigs that tickle your fancy. What did buyers like, or dislike, about them? What they say can give you clues to help you design a better gig, and position it, so more people will choose to do business with you.

You don't have to pick out your first gig right now, just jot down as many ideas as you can.

Study your list of possible gigs.

Draw a star by the ones you think would be a good fit for you. Cross off the ones you don't think would be a good fit for you, or you can't see yourself doing.

Okay. This is where the rubber meets the road. At this point, you should have at least five gigs you think would give you a great start on Fiverr.

Make sure the gigs you choose are something you can make money doing.

Most sellers agree to earn money you need to offer a service you can complete in no more than fifteen minutes. Five minutes or less is even better.

At fifteen minutes per gig, and an average profit of $4.00 per gig, that means you can make $16.00 per hour. If you can lower your working time to ten minutes per gig, you can make $24.00 per hour.

Now go back and evaluate the gig ideas you picked out. Be brutally honest.

Is this something you can do in fifteen minutes, or less? If not, is there a way you can do it faster? If not, scratch this gig off your list, or move it to your "needs work" pile.

Continue to evaluate each potential gig the same way.

If you're sure, you can complete them in fifteen minutes or less, great! Add them to your list of must do gigs.

The last step is to work a couple of your potential gigs to make sure how fast you can do them. Use a stopwatch to track your time. Make a list of your gigs by how much time they took you to complete.

"Don't skip this step," cautions Jon. "Every time I pass on testing, it comes back to bite me. Anymore, If I can't finish a gig in five to eight minutes, I say the hell with it.

"My goal is forty bucks an hour. If a gig doesn't let me make that, I shelve it, no matter how many sales I think I can make."

Pick the gig you want to get started on today.

From here on out we're going to concentrate on getting this gig ready to post on Fiverr.

Create your first gig

Posting a gig on Fiverr consists of nine simple steps.

For this demonstration, we're going to assume you're going to sell a Kindle book cover. As we walk through the steps, take some time to reflect on each step, and how the process relates to creating your gig.

One of my favorite book cover designers created the gig we're going to examine next. Right now, she has 86 orders in her queue, so you know this lady is breaking her ass to get them done. But at the same time, she's making some serious bucks.

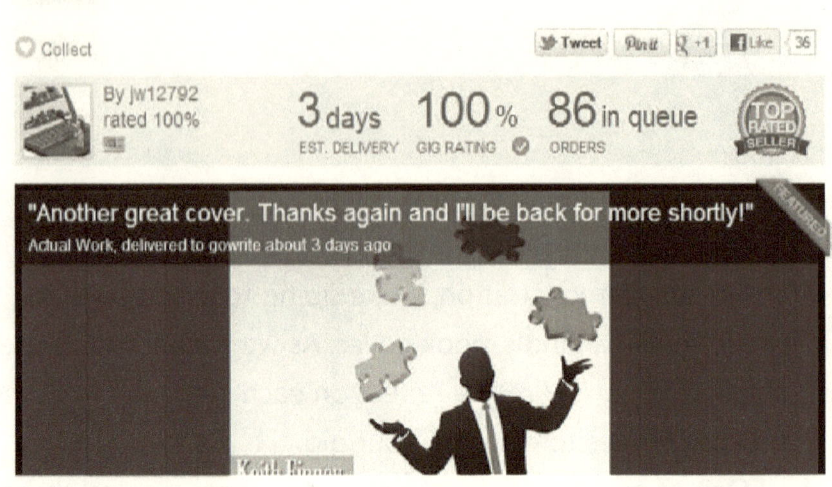

To get started, choose the Start Selling button at the top of Fiverr's main page.

Step 1. The first thing you're going to see are the familiar words, "I will ____ for $5.00." Now that gigs can start at more than five dollars it's no longer part of the form. You can still state the dollar amount if it gives you a one up on your competition.

Tell people what you're willing to do for $5.00. A good gig title should be short, tell people exactly what you are going to do for them, and be rich in keywords.

Look at the title of this gig. "I will design a professional and unique eBook cover or Kindle cover for $5.00."

It's a great title. It contains three main keywords "design," "eBook cover," and "Kindle cover." It also has two descriptors or adjectives "professional" and "unique."

The right keywords will give it an excellent shot at being picked up and shown by Fiverr's search engine every time someone searches for either "eBook cover" or "Kindle cover."

Step 2. Select a category. The beautiful thing here is Fiverr makes choosing a category super-easy. They only give you twelve choices: Fun & Bizarre, Online Marketing, Graphics and Design, Advertising, Writing & Translation, Lifestyle, Business, Programming & Tech, Other, Music & Audio, Gifts, and Video and Animation.

Pick the category that best describes your gig. It will give you the best bang for your buck.

Step 3. Description. Tell your story. Tell people what you are selling, what the benefits are for them, and what information you need from them to make it happen. If there are things you cannot, or will not do, this is the place to say it. A lot of sellers that offer art and writing services specify they won't write or draw pornography. Remember, it's your business, and what you choose to do, or not do, is up to you.

Let's look at the description in our sample listing.

"Over 5,000 covers created to date! 3D Covers are FREE, and when I say three days, I mean three days – regardless of

*the orders in the queue...and I'm not happy until you are so--UNLIMITED REVISIONS! Order now! * I also create covers for ALL genres, so let's hear what you have in mind. What makes my covers stand out from other designers here on Fiverr? I treat your cover as an individual! Are cars the theme of your book? How do metallic fonts and backgrounds sound? Chocolate the theme? We'll make book buyers want to lick the cover itself! Trust me; you'll love your cover. Order now!"*

What do you think?

This description offers so many examples of the things you should try to include for every one of your gigs. The seller tells you twice to "Order Now!" She tells you once in the middle, and again at the end.

She emphasizes her covers are different from those made by other designers on Fiverr. Then she tells you what makes them better and different – "We'll make book buyers want to lick the cover itself!"

She guarantees people who purchase her gig they will be pleased with their cover. "I'm not happy until you are so--UNLIMITED REVISIONS!"

Take some time to read through the descriptions written by many different Top Rated Sellers, and you'll quickly learn the secrets to being more successful and selling more gigs on Fiverr.

Step 4. Instructions to Buyer. Tell viewers what information you need to put their order together.

Fiverr uses this box to request information to help you complete the order, so before you fill it out, take a few minutes to carefully decide what information you need to make the project come together. The clearer you are with your instructions, the easier it will be to complete your project in as little time as possible.

Another benefit will be better feedback because you delivered your gig on time, and exactly how the buyer wanted it.

Step 5. Tags. Tags are simply a list of keywords people use to search for your gig on Fiverr.

ebook cover books design web kindle dsn

A simple way to pick your tags is to see what keywords other sellers are using to tag their gigs. Choose the keywords you think are relevant, and add them here.

Step 6. Maximum days to complete. What's the longest it will take you to deliver the finished gig? As a new seller, you should strive to complete every gig within twenty-four hours.

People like fast.

Everybody wants to buy something today and get it yesterday. Many buyers will choose your gig over someone else's when you offer one day service, especially when other sellers list a three to five-day turnaround.

Only offer one-day turnaround if you can deliver on it. You will hurt your rankings and increase your chances of receiving negative feedback if you deliver late. If you're unsure you can finish your gig in one day, determine how many days it will take you to complete your gig and then shoot to deliver it early whenever you can. That will give buyers a pleasant surprise, and happy buyers mean good reviews.

Step 7. Add image. Upload images to illustrate your gig. These should be the best samples of your work. For illustrations, Fiverr recommends a .jpeg format, 600 pixels wide x 370 pixels high, with a maximum file size of 5 megabytes. Once you have your pictures ready, you can use MS Paint or another graphics program to resize them to 600 x 370 pixels.

It is also recommended you upload a video. It can be something as simple as you talking about how you produce your gigs, giving instructions on the information you need from the seller to complete their order, or a collage showing your gigs and comments from the people who purchased them.

Keep it simple. Be informative. Better yet, make it humorous.

Step 8. This item requires shipping. If you are sending a physical product to buyers such as a small craft, check this box.

Step 9. Press the **Save** button.

Before you select save, take a few minutes to look it over first.

- Did you spell everything correctly?
- Did you include enough keywords in your title and description?
- Are your tags or keywords ones that buyers will use to search for your gig?
- Did you include all the information you're going to require in your information request line?

When you're happy with everything, press **Save** and your gig will go live.

Pretty simple, right?

Here are a few things you should keep in mind as you begin your career on Fiverr:

- Sellers can list a maximum of twenty gigs at one time. Choose the gigs you offer carefully. Make sure they are gigs you can complete the quickest, and that will sell the best.

- When you are first starting out, you're only allowed to offer two gig extras, but many sellers have found a workaround for this. They suggest buyers should purchase an additional gig if they want something extra. For example, if your gig is to write a 200-word

SEO article for $5.00, you could mention that buyers "should purchase an additional gig for every extra 200 words. It gives you the same benefit as offering a gig extra.

- Be careful about the types of gigs you offer. Reviews and testimonials are big business on Fiverr, but bogus book or product reviews for Amazon items is against Amazon's terms of service. What you will discover is many of these reviewers have a very short lifespan on Fiverr, because they quickly get shut down.

- Always offer a great value for the money you are charging. It will come back to you in good reviews and more business over the long haul.

- Spend at least a half-hour every week checking through the gigs offered on Fiverr. Try to spot new trends and services you may not currently be offering. New services will help you to grow your business, and keep your offerings fresh and relevant.

Fiverr Selling 101

Fiverr continues to reinvent itself, as the freelance marketplace evolves. Gigs are no longer required to start at $5.00, but most buyers offer a $5.00 gig as a gateway to more expensive offerings.

"Five dollars is the sweet spot to reel buyers in," says Martin.

"When you start at five dollars, more people look at your gig. Position it right. Create great gig extras and package attributes, and you will make the big bucks.

"All my listings start at five dollars, but my average sale is $22.00. Take that times 273 sales a month and life is good. Very good!"

We've already talked about gig extras. Depending upon your seller level they give you an incredible opportunity to boost your income while customizing your gigs to meet buyer wants and needs.

Package attributes is a relatively new feature that can boost your sales.

If you've spent any time on Fiverr, you probably know what I'm talking about—even if you don't recognize the name.

	$5 Basic	$10 Standard	$15 Premium
Description	Basic Package A front cover of the book	Premium Package A front cover, back cover and spine of the book	Pro Package A front cover, back cover, spine and 3D image of the book
Back & Side	–	✔	✔
3D Image	–	–	✔
Delivery Time	2 days 1 day (+$5)	3 days 1 day (+$10)	3 days 1 day (+$10)
	Select $5	Select $10	Select $15

What I like about package attributes is they make it easy for buyers to compare your offerings. You can offer a starter product for $5.00, a step-up for $25.00, and a bigger step-up for $50.00. Most sellers are going to pick the middle option. They don't want to go too cheap, but they don't want to blow their whole wad either.

Package attributes make it easier to convert lookers into buyers because you're offering them more choices. I don't have any definite proof, but my guess is package attributes convert better than gig extras.

Experiment with your listings, and discover what works best for you.

"You are crazy if you're not using package attributes," says Jon. "It's the best way sellers have to up-sell their gig. If you're not using them, you are leaving money on the table. Lots of money."

Custom Offers[1] are where you can make the real money. *Forbes Magazine*[2] did a story about four sellers who make $15,000 a month, or more, by using custom offers. One of the ladies profiled in the article runs an executive resume writing service. She went from making $5.00 per gig to making over $300,000 last year. A lot of her business comes from creating custom resume packages and selling them for $500 to $800 each—all by sending custom offers.

Think you can't do it? Think again.

Suppose you're a graphic artist selling custom book covers on eBay. Create the listing just as you normally would. Add package attributes and gig extras to upsell regular buyers. The only thing I want you to do differently is to add an additional line at the top and bottom of your item description page. It can be as simple as, "looking for something extra-special? Contact me for a Custom Offer."

That throws it back into the buyer's court. Some of them are going to be curious, and contact you. When they do,

---

1 http://blog.fiverr.com/custom-offers-taking-business-next-level/

2 http://www.forbes.com/sites/laurashin/2016/05/31/how-these-3-people-make-6-figures-a-year-on-fiverr/#346bbb383ee5

ask some discovery questions, and fire off an offer to let them know what you can do for them.

Fiverr Anywhere[3] works hand in hand with Custom Offers to help you make larger dollar sales.

Fiverr Anywhere started out as a Google Chrome extension. Since then it was moved to the Fiverr site. To access *Fiverr Anywhere* go to the Promote Your Business section under the My Sales Tab. Click on the Generate Custom Offer tab, then create your custom offer. After you've done that, you can retrieve your link. That will let you add your offer to your website, blog, email, or social media sites.

When someone contacts you, it works just like a regular Custom Offer. Potential buyers can accept your offer, or request a modification.

Use *Fiver Anywhere* and *Custom Offer* to grow your business and reach new customers off the Fiverr website.

Good-luck! And, great selling on Fiverr!

---

[3] http://blog.fiverr.com/take-fiverr-business-anywhere/

Workbook # 1

Make Your Title Sell Your Gig

Think of your gig title as your elevator pitch.

You get 80 characters to tell people about your gig, what it can do for them, and why you're the best guy to do it.

Nail this, and you're going to make a lot of sales. Get it wrong, and you're going to be asking yourself, "What went wrong?"

The *Fiverr Academy*[4] suggests the most important part of writing your gig title is to ensure you create the proper gig URL. When you do this, it optimizes the SEO ranking to give you an edge over your competition.

Their thought is writing your title should be a two-step process. Your first title should focus on creating the proper URL. Then you write a title that grabs buyer's attention.

Doing this gives you the biggest bang for your buck.

---

[4] https://www.fiverr.com/academy/tips-tricks/seo-tricks-for-gig-titles

Here's how it works.

An SEO driven title says what you will do. "Create Kindle eBook cover." The resulting gig URL would be "username create-Kindle-eBook-cover."

It's not reader friendly, but it's guaranteed to draw a lot of search engine traffic.

Now, you can come back to your title, and share a story that's going to resonate with buyers searching for your services.

It used to be all titles began with the words, "I will____for $5.00." Now that gigs can start at more than $5.00, titles start with, "I will____."

It's up to you to fill in the blanks.

Every seller has their opinion of what to include in the title.

Jon says, "Make sure you mention how long it takes you to complete the job. People want their stuff fast. Often, they will choose you, over the next guy if you can deliver your work quicker."

"The title needs to tell buyers exactly what they will get," says Mohammed. "Most people don't bother to read the description. They read the title. They look at your feedback, and they may give your gig a quick read through, but that's all you can expect—especially if you're doing graphic design work. People just want to see what you can do, and how soon you're going to deliver."

No wonder there is so much confusion.

Sellers deliver what their gig promises, buyers often expect something entirely different because they didn't bother to read the entire terms and conditions.

Language is another problem area.

More than 80 percent of buyers are from the United States, but 70 percent of sellers come from outside of the United States.

That's a recipe for disaster.

Here's the best advice I can give.

Short is better.

You've got eighty characters to tell people what you will do, but you don't want to say too much.

People have a short attention span.

If you say too much, it's just going to confuse them; then they will move on to the next listing.

Eight to ten words are best.

Say what you will do.

Sprinkle in two or three keywords—any more is too much. If you are doing book cover design, stick with the basics—Kindle, eBook cover, and CreateSpace. If you write blog posts, consider—SEO writing, article writing.

If you have any doubts about which keywords to use, check what your competition is doing.

Ordinarily, you wouldn't mention delivery time, but if you're a new seller and everybody else has three-day or seven-day delivery, you could score a lot of quick sales by offering 24-hour delivery in your title.

If other sellers in your category provide one or two revisions, use your title to differentiate yourself—offer "unlimited revisions." Sellers who are on edge may choose you because of past problems resolving issues.

"Whenever I start a new gig, I look for ways to distinguish myself," says Holly. "Then I make sure I list the key differentiators in my title."

You never know what's going to grab somebody's attention. If your first title doesn't sell as many gigs as you hoped for—change it.

Keep shaking things up until you get the sales you want.

Workbook # 2

Craft a Picture or Video That Sells Your Gig

One of the more important and most underused spots on the gig description page is the gig video or picture.

So many sellers decide video is too hard or too complicated, and they don't want to bother with finding the perfect picture because it's too much work.

Big mistake.

An awesome video can make the difference between a so-so gig and a virtual cash machine.

Video sells.

If you have any doubts, check out YouTube or Facebook. The most liked and viewed posts are cutesie videos of babies, pets, and people in crazy situations.

If you want to rocket your gig to the top of Fiverr, you need a video. But, not just any video.

You need to create a video that captures the essence of your offer.

"I recommend talking about your gig," says Jon. "Don't overcomplicate things. Explain your offer. Tell potential buyers what makes you different from your competition."

Jorge says, "It's not so much what you say, but how you come across on your video. What you want to do is show buyers you're a real person who is passionate about their work and will do whatever it takes to get it right.

"Done right, a video is your best sales tool. I shoot all of mine from my iPhone. They're not as professional as some of the other ones you see on Fiverr, but they're authentic, and that's what buyers want to see.

"It tells them I'm the guy."

Make sure your video says what makes you better than other sellers?

- Are you a product knowledge expert?
- Have you been working at the same business since the dawn of time?
- Did you write the go-to book on what you're doing?
- Did you win a major award? Or even some obscure local award for what you do?
- Are you a **Top-Rated Seller**, or the number one seller in your category?

Mention as many of these things as you can in your gig video. If you're still at a loss about what to include, show a sample of your work.

If nothing else, show people you are real. Give them a glimpse of your personality. Let them know you want to help them.

If you're still stumped, keep it simple. Use your smartphone camera to record your first videos.

- Give your name, then give a short pitch for your gig.
- Create a different video for each gig.
- Say your offer is only available on Fiverr. I'm not sure why, but it creates a certain amount of exclusivity by letting buyers know they can't find it anywhere else.
- Don't waste time. Get right to the point.
- Focus on the solution you are offering

Here's the tech talk.

1. 30 seconds is the minimum length for a video
2. 60 seconds is the maximum length for a video
3. Maximum video size is 50 MB
4. Accepted file formats are MP4 and AVI
5. For more information on uploading and using gig videos check out this link. http://support.fiverr.com/hc/en-us/articles/201500946-Adding-a-Video-to-Your-Gig

If you use a picture, and you should—keep these facts in mind.

- You can upload one video, and three pictures
- Photos should be in JPEG format or JPG format, and no larger than 5 MB
- Recommended picture size is 550 x 370 pixels

Be sure your images are relevant to the gig. Nothing is more frustrating for buyers than being forced to view illustrations that don't apply to the subject at hand. Not only is it confusing; it makes them wonder what service the seller is offering. If they can't figure it out quickly, they're going to choose another gig.

The best pictures are samples of completed gigs or a collage of gig photos.

"I've seen a lot of clip art illustrations, side by side with a picture of the seller at their desk or holding their laptop with a short quote about the gig superimposed on the picture," says Jon. "It's very effective, especially if the seller is a cute young girl."

Book cover and logo designers have gig pictures down to an art. Many of them have created gallery pictures or collages that feature fifteen or twenty samples of their work. The result is a very convincing sales page that quickly shows potential buyers what they can do.

Workbook # 3

Gig Descriptions Are All About Them

Gig descriptions are all about your customer.

You only get a few seconds to catch someone's attention, so your heading and first few sentences are going to be make or break.

Don't talk too much about your gig. Instead, let people know you understand their problem—that you feel their pain. After that, you can explain how your gig will help them ease their suffering.

Here's a great example from Lauria. It recognizes the customer's pain point (dilemma), then explains how they can help.

> *If you are an* ***author*** *or a* ***publisher****, then you surely know that all eBooks need an* ***amazing cover****. Let's be Honest. Books with good graphic, and* ***eye-catching fonts*** *sell*

more copies.

Our Job is to make sure that your eBook covers stand out, ***we're not satisfied with your cover until you are.***

This example is from Ravsingh, a Level 2 seller. It's a good example of how to introduce yourself, and brand you as an expert.

> *I've been designing eBook covers and other graphic related items for over* ***seven years*** *and have worked with customers from over* ***70 countries****.*
>
> *In this gig, I offer a unique and* ***professional*** *cover design for your eBook. Your cover will be* ***100% unique.*** *I never use any pre-made templates of any kind. You will receive your cover within 24 hours.*
>
> *Each order comes with free revisions (rounds of changes) after your cover is delivered so you can make it perfect.*
>
> *Order now and let me know if have any questions, I'm always happy to help! Thanks :)*

Each description makes good use of bold to highlight key points. Ravsingh works in the Keywords: eBook and covers.

Lauria uses the Keywords: eBook and cover design. Further down in the description, they include "Kindle and CreateSpace." Lauria also highlights the advantages of using them. They offer "100% unique" designs, "24-hour" delivery, and "free revisions."

Remember, white space is your friend.

Most people don't read. Potential buyers are going to skim through your description so they can quickly find the information they need.

Use bold headlines and bullet points whenever possible. Present your information logically.

1. Talk about the problem you're going to solve.
2. Introduce yourself, and your gig. Then tell people how you're going to solve their problem.
3. Tell customers what's unique about your gig. There are a million and one SEO gigs on Fiverr. What makes your gig different? Why should someone buy from you, instead of the guy with twenty-thousand feedbacks? If you can't answer that question, you need to reexamine your gig.
4. You need to get up close and personal with buyers. Use "you" and "your." When you use those two words, it makes it easier for buyers to connect with you.
5. Inject some of your personality into each of your gigs—humor—faith—whatever it is that keeps you going. Share something about yourself.

6. Spelling and grammar are important. Fiverr is riddled with poor grammar, frequent misspellings, and misused words. It's easy to understand why. As I said earlier, 80 percent of buyers are American, 70 percent of sellers are from somewhere else. That's bound to create problems. My best advice is if you're not a native English speaker, find someone who is. Pay them to translate your gig. It may not be as important for SEO or design gigs, but if your gig focuses on writing or editing services, spelling mistakes, and bad grammar are going to stop you dead in your tracks.

When in doubt, put yourself in your buyer's shoes. Find out what they want, need, and are willing to pay for and give it to them.

I know it's been said before, but it bears repeating: It's not about you; it's about your customers. Focus on what they want. Give it to them, and you will have more business than you can handle.

After you've been in business a while and your gig is a big success you need to shake things up a bit.

Change your gig description. Tell potential buyers how many satisfied customers you have. Let them know you have twenty-thousand feedbacks. Change your delivery time. If you've got two or three hundred orders in your queue, customers are going to understand it's going to take some time to deliver their order. Some will try out the new guy so they can get their order quicker, but most of them will wait. They want the best. They will balance time and money against the finished product. And, if they need it now, they will pay the extra ten or twenty bucks for super-fast delivery. That's why Fiverr invented gig extras.

Final Thoughts: Even though not everyone reads it, your description is essential. It's the go-to spot for customers who are on the line about whether to purchase your gig or not. If something goes wrong (and it will) your description can be used to help resolve the problem. It serves as the starting point to determine what you promised, what the customer received, and the difference between the two.

To prevent any misunderstandings, ensure your description is clear, concise, and easy to understand. You will thank yourself later.

Workbook # 4

Custom Offers Will Take Your Business to a New Level

What would you think if I told you, you could quadruple or quintuple your Fiverr income by doing just one thing?

Would you be interested?

And, what if I told you, it wouldn't take much more effort than you are investing right now. Would you be interested?

Of course, you would, right?

What I'm talking about is Fiverr's new *Custom Offer* feature. It's this nifty new tool that lets you create custom packages targeted towards a buyer's individual wants and needs.

Not too long ago *Forbes Magazine*[5] published an article about an executive resume writer who took her income from several thousand dollars per month to thirty thousand dollars per month. By sending highly targeted *Custom*

[5] http://www.forbes.com/sites/laurashin/2016/05/31/how-these-3-people-make-6-figures-a-year-on-fiverr/#346bbb383ee5

Offers to business executives, she increased her average gig revenue to $800.

Not bad, for writing a resume.

Another seller on Fiverr's website[6] said he talked to a client about making money online, and the next thing he knew he was sending them a *Custom Offer* to give a personalized presentation to their customers.

How cool is that?

What baffles me, though, is when I receive *Custom Offers* from sellers who think small.

Last week I received *Custom Offers* from two sellers who offered me a book promotion gig. They promised to promote my book to what seemed like six bazillion people for just $5.00.

That doesn't even make sense.

If they went to all the bother to search completed gigs on Fiverr to find potential customers, why would they make such a wimpy offer?

Book promotions go for big bucks.

Many times, I've spent $400 or $500 on a single book campaign. The larger websites like BookBub charge upwards of $250. FreeBooksy costs $75 or higher, and BargainBooksy starts at $25.

If the person making the *Custom Offer* knows their business, they should know what similar companies are charging. If that's the case, why are they offering a five dollar service when they could easily charge $25 or $100?

---

[6] http://blog.fiverr.com/custom-offers-taking-business-next-level/

It's an example of what I would call the think small and grovel syndrome.

Honestly, *Custom Offers* are a great way to boost your income, but to take advantage of them, you've got to think big. You need to understand your category, your customer's pain points, and how your services can help customers relieve their pain and suffering.

Think of yourself as a doctor.

If you copyedit and proofread manuscripts, you need to look at the big-picture. Instead of just editing for spelling and grammar errors, what other services would benefit your customers?

Could you analyze their documents and ensure they are following the correct stylesheet? Could you annotate their manuscript and let them know if they failed to introduce a new character? Or, maybe you could let them know they forgot to footnote a quote or fact?

Sometimes, a writer just needs another unbiased eye on his manuscript to tell him (or her) what works, or what doesn't work and why. Sometimes, an extra set of eyes on a manuscript can make all the difference.

Every time you receive an order or inquiry, you could follow up with a *Custom Offer* that details what other services you offer. Maybe, you only receive one order for every ten or fifteen *Custom Offers* you send out but say it brings in an extra $250 in revenue.

Is it worth it? Would it change your business? Would it change your lifestyle?

So, what's the best way to get started using *Custom Offers*?

First off, sellers need to understand Fiverr limits how many *Custom Offers* you can send each day. *Level One* sellers can send three offers a day; *Level Two* sellers can send ten.

Other than that, there are several ways to get started.

1. Some sellers send them to everyone who places a new order. The best way to do this is to look at what your customer ordered, the buyer's previous order history on Fiverr, and then think about how you can add value. If the purchaser is an author, visit their Amazon author page. Do they have Kindle, paperback, and audiobooks for each of their titles? Send them a *Custom Offer* for all three. It might not work, but with just a little more effort on your part, it gives you a chance to triple your income in each order.

2. A lot of buyers troll the gig request list. When they find one they can do, they shoot off a *Custom Offer*. The advantage here is if you're a new seller, not having feedback isn't a problem. Buyers can't see your ranking, so it doesn't work against you when you send a *Custom Offer*. The only thing I would advise is not to link to one of your gigs, instead, tailor a deal for each offer. And, for God's sake, charge more than $5.00. You're worth it.

3. Use *Fiverr Anywhere* to post deals on your website, blog, social media sites, and in targeted email campaigns. Doing this gives you the best chance to get your offer out there to anyone who may benefit from it.

Example 1. *Hi, I'm Jill from the US. I'm working on facebook and other social medias with promotion campaigns. I can help you to promote your kindle book in facebook. In this offer, I will do my "Large page promotion" extra for free with my basic gig. Also I'm giving extra fast delivery for free!!This is a good offer, and it is for limited period. Please order my gig. Hope to give you the best result. Thank you!*

It's obvious; this seller should have given this *Custom Offer* some more thought before sending it out. The misspellings and grammatical mistakes make it apparent the offer isn't worth the five dollars the seller is asking.

A better proposal would read something like this.

> *Hi, I'm Jill from the United States. I'm an expert in Facebook, Twitter, and Pinterest marketing, and can help promote your Kindle eBook. I've been helping author's launch new books for over five years now, and have played an integral part in moving over fifty titles to number one in their category. While I can't make any promises, I guarantee I will do my best to get your book moving up the charts.*

Do you see the difference?

It's well written, engaging, and everything in it works to position the seller as an expert in book marketing. The first Custom Offer would have had a hard time getting anyone to spend five dollars; the second one could easily have asked for fifty to one hundred dollars because it built value into it.

> *Example 2. Hi, I'm John, and I've been a resume writer on Fiverr for over six months now. No matter what industry you're searching in, I can write the perfect resume. Need a new cover letter? I can help with that, too.*

Not bad. But not good, either.

What do you think of this one?

> *Good Morning. My name is John. I've worked as a career counselor and resume specialist for the last twenty-five years. I ensure high-level executives in the telecommunications field make the best first impression with their resumes and cover letters. I do things a little different than most sellers on Fiverr. I get to know you, your goals, and what you want to accomplish before I start working. That way you get a resume and cover letter tailored to your career goals. It's a different way of doing business on Fiverr, but the results speak for themselves. My feedback is*

impeccable, but if you have any questions or concerns, I'd be happy to address them before we get started.

What do you think?

Would you buy from John? Of course, you would, because he's the real deal. In less than 100 words, he positioned himself as an industry expert, and the guy you would want to have on your side in any job search campaign.

If you want to take your custom offers to the next level—tailor them to your customer's wants, needs, and desires. You will hit more home runs when you do it this way.

Workbook # 5

Promote Your Fiverr Gigs

Sellers are all over the board about how to promote your Fiverr gigs.

Some insist you need to blow up social media; others suggest you should troll forums on Facebook, LinkedIn, Quora, Yahoo Answers, etc. While still others, say you need to seed your gigs and have friends make the first few purchases and leave five-star reviews to get you off to a good start.

Who is right? Who is wrong?

All of them are. I wrote the book on social media marketing, and I can tell you—all these ideas work—some of the time—and for some of the people.

It all comes down to your style, how many followers you have, and how engaged you are with your following.

Personally, I'm horrible at talking to people face-to-face. I'm even worse at social media and blogging because I can't commit to making regular posts.

I'm good at getting started, but follow up kicks my butt.

The guys that are good with social media, blogging and trolling forums are good at it because they commit to a regular schedule. They post on social media at regular times every day. They post articles on their blog on the same day—at the same time—every week.

Why?

People get used to it.

Over time, they will check back on the same day and time to see what's next. Once you've got them hooked they will keep coming back, time-after-time, unless you let them down.

So, if you want to harness the power of social media to drive sales to your Fiverr gigs, you know what to do.

If you're like me, and want to put your gigs on autopilot, and let Fiverr do all the heavy-lifting for you, you're going to like this part.

On Page Optimization

To be successful on Fiverr or anywhere on the web, you need to optimize your sales page. That way you put the power of the website and Google behind you.

Fiverr's sale page consists of three major parts—title, gig picture (video)—and description.

Title

An SEO focused title is your best sales tool. If you get it right, over time, it's going to bring a boatload of organic traffic from Google, Yahoo, Bing, and other search engines.

The Fiverr blog put it best when they said writing your title is a two-part process.

Your first title is all about SEO. It creates your gig URL (what shows up when you conduct a Google search).

You need to talk about your gig. Keep it short, simple, and to the point.

Say what you're going to do.

1. Create Kindle eBook cover
2. Write SEO optimized blog post
3. Proofread copyedit manuscript
4. Create design website banner
5. Custom whiteboard explainer video

Do you understand the reason behind setting up your title URL first?

It's how buyers search for you online. They leave out all unessential words and just type in the bare basics of what they're looking for. If that doesn't get the results they want, they add more keywords to their search terms.

What you need to do is think like a customer.

What keywords are they likely to search by? Are they going to search for Kindle or eBook? Are they going to search for whiteboard or explainer? Are they going to search for proofreading or copyediting?

It's not so easy, is it?

Everyone is different.

Everyone explains things differently. Some people know what they want, but they're unsure what it's called. Other people aren't sure what they want, they just have a general idea—video—voiceover—Facebook.

You've got to get enough keywords in your URL so everyone of them can find you.

After you've nailed your SEO title, you need to write the people friendly version.

It's going to need a little more oomph to draw their attention. You need to keep the keywords, but you've got to punch it up a little. Make it sound exciting. Fun. New. Creative. Unique.

To do that you've got to use some adjectives. Funny as it is, Fiverr is the only website where I'd recommend padding your title by adding some adjectives.

So, what does a good title sound like?

1. I will create custom Whiteboard Doodle Animation Explainer
2. I will create a unique EXPLAINER video in only 24 hours
3. I will make you a custom video with Professor Puppet
4. I will write an effective SEO article of 300 to 500 words

5. I will write a unique SEO article – 500 words in 24 hours
6. I will write a professional jingle, record it with vocals and guitar

Remember, your title is a fluid creation.

Monitor your results. If you're not getting the sales you want, shake things up a bit. Move the words around. Switch one word for another. Change your keywords.

If your title is too long, make it shorter.

If it isn't working altogether, go back to the drawing board. Examine what the Top-Rated Sellers in your category are doing. Don't steal their titles. Instead, follow their example. Use some of the keywords they're using. If you're new to the category, stress that you offer 24-hour, or super-quick delivery.

Gig Video/Picture

We've already talked about this one, but let's give it another quick look.

Any video will give you a boost up over 90 percent of your competition. A well-thought out and original video will change the direction of your Fiverr gigs.

I'm a writer.

When I created my proofreading and copyediting gigs, I stressed that in my gig video. I placed some of my books on my desk so viewers could see them as I talked. If I'd been smart, I would have hung a couple of poster boards of my book covers in the background. They would have spoken louder than any words I said.

When you make your video, it doesn't need to be a full-on professional production. It needs to be authentic. It needs to reach out and slap buyers in the face and make them say: "Yeah! He's the guy (or gal)."

Select your background. Fire up your iPhone camera, and begin talking. Don't read some long, drawn-out script, just talk about your gig.

Fiverr only gives you 30 to 60 seconds, so don't waste time. Go right to the meat of your offer.

Look in to the camera. Smile. Introduce yourself, then talk about your gig. Say what you will do. Why you're the best person to do it. Stress the value and quality you are offering.

Post your video on YouTube, then Fiverr. When you post it on YouTube, write a short keyword focused description, and be sure to add a link to your gig.

If you're unsure of the video requirements here's a quick recap. Fiverr requires videos to be between 30 and 60 seconds long, under 50 megabytes, and submitted in MP4 or AVI format.

Gig Pictures

Fiverr lets sellers add one video and up to three photos for each gig.

Whatever you do, don't just slap up any old picture. Make sure it relates to your gig and helps buyers visualize your offering.

Graphic designers have it easier here.

They can post pictures of previously completed gigs. If they're just starting out, they can create several mock-ups and post them.

The rest of us need to think outside of the box. You can post a picture of yourself. If buyers permit it, you can post a picture of them or their completed gig along with highlights of their feedback.

I've seen copyeditors, and proofreaders post a picture of themselves alongside an illustration of a pen and a manuscript. One lady included a pull quote from her gig description under her picture.

Your illustrations don't have to be fancy or professionally done. They just need to capture the essence of your gig. A good photo reinforces the title and helps to build confidence that you're the guy.

Just like the video, you need to use different pictures for each of your gigs. If you're not getting the sales you need switch it up a little. Pay a Fiverr designer to create something unique and relevant to what you do. Your investment will pay off over the long haul.

Description

Similar to the title, the description has a dual objective.

It needs to be keyword rich so that spiders can easily find and index the information on your page. Don't go overboard. Mention your main keywords once or twice in the description, anymore, and it will appear like you're keyword spamming.

If you check what Top-Rated Sellers are doing, many of them highlight or bold-face their keywords. SEO *gurus* say search engines put extra emphasis on bold, highlighted, and underlined words.

If you do this, you're going to draw more organic traffic to your sales page. Eventually, if enough people search for and click on your gig, it will move up in search.

The goal is to get to the top ten searches for your gig. People are lazy. Less than half of them will explore beyond the first page of search results.

When you write your description for people, you need to create it the way people read on the web.

They don't read, they skim.

If you've got a big long chunk of text buyers are going to do one of two things. Either they're going to click out of your description, or they're going to buy it sight unseen.

Neither result is good.

If a buyer clicks away from your sales page, you lose the sale. If they buy without reading your full description, that means they might not get what they want. If that happens you could get bad feedback.

Whitespace is your friend.

Begin with a short, bold-faced headline. Follow it up with a brief paragraph composed of no more than two or three sentences. Then use a series of bullet points to highlight the details of your offering.

Be sure to say what your basic gig does and does not include. If you offer gig extras, explain what buyers get with each of them, and why they would want to choose it.

1. "Extra fast delivery moves your order to the top of our queue and ensures that you will receive your order within 24 hours."

2. "Add the CreateSpace option, and I will create a back cover and spine to go with your book cover."

Claim your profile

The final step in optimizing and promoting your gig is to fill out your seller profile like a pro.

A lot of sellers don't do this. They don't think anybody looks at it so—why bother?

Big mistake!

When sellers are on the line or wavering about whether to buy or not, many of them turn to your profile page. It gives them a little more information about you—your qualifications, education, experience, and personality.

If you don't do anything else, upload a photo and fill out your description.

Keep it short and sweet.

Here's my Fiverr profile.

> *Nick Vulich writes short, easy to read books that challenge reader's minds and help them understand the world around them. He's written several category bestsellers on Amazon including eBay 2014, eBay 2015, eBay 2016, E-commerce 2017, History Bytes, and Shot All to Hell. Put his writing, copyediting, and proofreading skills to work on your next project.*

It gives some quick information about me and my books, then it gets down to business and invites readers to use my services. Do something similar in your profile. Inject some of your personality, experience, or awards. Talk about what makes you unique, and the best guy for the job.

Fiverr has several hundred thousands sellers. Fill out your Profile as completely as possible. It's another way to make you stand out and make more sales.

The remainder of the Profile page lets you add your skills, languages, certifications, social media accounts, and education.

Bonus Excerpt – Social Media Marketing Made Easy

(Here's an excerpt from my book, Kill it With Social Media. *This section focuses on how to use Social Media, especially Twitter, and LinkedIn. I changed some of the wording and examples so that this sample is more relevant to the needs of Fiverr merchants.)*

Social Media Marketing for eBay Sellers

Do you need to blow up social media to sell on Fiverr and other e-commerce sites?

Its sort of like asking, are you a glass is half full, or glass is half empty type of person. If you're a glass is half full type, you're going to scream "Damn right! You have to be on social media, because—that's where the people are." If you're a glass is half empty type you're going to piss and moan "What's the point? I'm selling my stuff on Fiverr, not on Facebook and Twitter."

You probably see where I'm going with this.

Online sellers are divided on the need for social media, its uses, and its outcomes. Some vendors will tell you they couldn't have gotten where they are without it; others will say "Why bother!" or "Hey! I tried it, and it didn't make any diff. My sales stayed the same."

I'm going to try not to take sides here. My goal is to give you the information you need to implement social media in your Fiverr business should you choose to do so.

My primary focus is going to be on Facebook, Twitter, LinkedIn, and Pinterest because they are the powerhouses of social media today. Facebook and Twitter get a bigger mention because they are the social media sites everybody uses. Pinterest gets a longer mention because it is the one sellers say works best. LinkedIn gets space because it's the place professionals meet to share information, exchange ideas, contact other professionals in their field, and to search for new business leads.

Does that mean you need to use all of them? Or that you should focus exclusively on Pinterest because it's what works best for most sellers? No. You should start out slow. Pick one or two social media platforms and spend ten or fifteen minutes on them two or three days a week.

A *PEW University* study on social media usage provides one more relevant piece of information for savvy online marketers—over half of the people who visit social media sites are active on more than one site. For marketers, the implication is clear if you want to reach your primary customer base, you need to be active on several social media platforms. Using one social media platform isn't going to cut it. Think a minimum of two, maybe even three social media platforms, if you want to reach your target audience.

When you are first getting started, watch what other sellers in businesses like yours do on social media. Like some of their posts and start building your network. Create a few short posts. Put up a few pictures, or some short videos. Rinse and repeat.

The key to success with social media is to post regularly, comment when someone likes or comments on one of your posts, and keep a conversation going with your followers. Over time you will develop a following of your own.

Don't try to move too quickly, or fast-track your way to success. There are a lot of merchants on Fiverr who sell 500 or 1,000 Facebook and Twitter likes. Don't be tempted. Phantom fans who don't comment on your posts, or like them, aren't going to do your business any good over the long haul.

Remember, it's not a contest to see who can get the most followers. It's all about getting the most followers who will engage with you on a regular basis, and who will share your content with their friends and followers.

That's how you build your business using social media. Give more than you get, share content your followers like, enjoy, and can use. If you do this, sales will follow.

Social Media by the Numbers

A PEW University[7] study published in 2014, says Seventy-one percent of adults who use the Internet are on Facebook. Twitter, LinkedIn, Instagram, and Pinterest lag way behind with adult usage rates that fall somewhere between 23 to 28 percent.

---

[7] http://www.pewinternet.org/2015/01/09/social-media-update-2014/

Here are a few key takeaways for anyone planning to use social media to grow their online business.

- 31 percent of seniors are on Facebook.
- 53 percent of young adults age 18 to 29 are on Instagram. And, over half of these users visit the site daily.
- Women are three times more likely to use Pinterest than men. 42 percent of women who use the internet are on Pinterest, versus 13 percent of men.

If you need more help in choosing the correct social media platform to reach your key demographics, check out the rest of the PEW University study.[8]

Facebook users are aging with a larger percentage of seniors over age sixty-five on the site. Women are more likely to frequent Facebook than men.

Twitter usage is higher among young adults ages eighteen to twenty-nine and falls off sharply among users at age forty-nine. Young adults and Afro-Americans are more likely to engage on Twitter.

Instagram has a high usage rate among young Americans ages eighteen to twenty-nine, and among Afro-Americans.

Pinterest users are primarily women, who tend to be college educated and more affluent.

LinkedIn is used less than other social media sites but could be helpful if you are marketing to individuals between the ages of fifty to sixty-five. LinkedIn users also

---

[8] http://www.pewinternet.org/2013/12/30/demographics-of-key-social-networking-platforms/

tend to be college graduates, with a higher annual household income.

The PEW University study does leave out one important group—teenagers.

If you're marketing primarily to teens, you need to check out a 2014 study by Piper Jaffray ... Taking Stock With Teens – Fall 2014.[9]

Here is some of the information you will discover.

- Your message better look good on an iPhone, because 67 percent of teenagers either have or plan on getting an iPhone.
- Instagram and Twitter are the social media site most frequented by teens. So, if teens are your target audience, you need to include more pictures, video, and music in your posts, and fewer words.
- Pinterest is the least used social media site among teens.
- Facebook is used by fifty percent of all teens but is not as popular as it was in the past.

One more important concept online sellers need to grasp is the people you want to reach are online a good portion of the day. Many of them rarely if ever leave social media sites, so if you don't engage with them there, you are not going to sell to them—period.

---

[9] http://www.piperjaffray.com/3col.aspx?id=3268

Twitter

For those of you not familiar with Twitter, it's the social media site that has the little blue bird as its mascot. When you feel compelled to communicate with the outside world, you send out a *tweet.*

Tweets are short, sweet, and to the point. There's no room for fluff or excess verbiage. You get 140 characters to tell your story, so you better boil it down to the essentials, and make every character count.

Another cool thing about Twitter is you can share pictures, videos, and links. In fact, if you don't include some visual element in your tweets, the odds are no one is going to bother with them. Sorry, but that's another rule of the game. Get over it.

On the face of things, Twitter would appear to be the easiest social media site to master. I mean, you only have 140 characters to tell your story.

If only it were so simple.

The way Twitter works, your message is only seen by your followers and other Twitter users with nothing better to do than searching the Twitterverse all day for trending topics.

Your topic is trending, isn't it?

We'll get to that in a bit. For now, the very least you need to know is Twitter is one of the social media powerhouses. Twitter says they have 288 million users who send out 500 million tweets every day. Many of these users send out as many as fifty to one hundred tweets per day.

Twitter's about page[10] gives us two other key pieces of intelligence.

- 80 percent of Twitter users visit the site via mobile. That means every tweet you send needs to be mobile friendly, and every link you include in your tweets needs to look good on the small screen of a smartphone or iPhone.
- 77 percent of Twitter users are outside of the United States which means there is a potentially huge communications gap. Many of the people who receive your tweets aren't going to understand what you're saying, so the visual element better tells your entire story. If it doesn't, you're wasting your time.

With that many tweets going out every day you can understand how easy it is to get lost in the clutter. Later in this section, I'll give you some tips to cut through the noise, and make your tweets easier to find.

Twitter 101

Twitter is a form of microblogging.

---

[10] https://about.twitter.com/company

Conversations on Twitter take place in real time and whittle the conversation down to short 140 character bursts.

The advantage to users is that it is instantaneous and occurs in real time. A lot of the breaking news stories you see on Headline News originate on Twitter.

Here's the scenario. A lone gunman attacks a school or business. Trapped students capture footage on their cell phones and post it to Twitter. Moments later it's picked up by network news and spread across the media.

Another scenario that plays out every year during storm season is someone captures footage of a tornado roaring by their home as they are headed for the storm cellar. Minutes later the video hits Twitter, then it's uploaded to Facebook, the local news station's website, and next thing you know, there's a viral video of the storm tossing a car into a tree or the house next door.

That's the nature of Twitter. As soon as something happens, you can have it online within seconds.

The good thing is disaster videos aren't the only ones that go viral. You can shoot a quick video of yourself or a customer talking about your business and post it all over YouTube and Twitter.

The Least You Need to Know

You can open a personal or business Twitter account. There is little difference between the two.

Next, you need to edit your profile. A lot of businesses skip this step.

Big mistake!

At the very least you need to add your company name, contact info, links to your blog—website, or other social media accounts, a profile photo, and a short one line bio. Other than your contact info the most important stuff you enter here is your bio. It tells people who you are, why you're on Twitter, and how you can help them.

My author bio on Twitter is short, sweet, and says all you need to know about me—"Short easy to read solutions to your e-commerce problems."

It's just 128 characters long but gives readers a good idea of what to expect. Create your bio the same way. Twitter gives you 160 characters to introduce yourself, make an impression, and convince visitors to click on your links. Spend the time you need to craft an amazing bio.

Twitter also gives you an opportunity to upload a theme to help brand your page.

Twitter recommends 1500 x 500 pixels as the ideal size for your header, but you can upload any theme you like between the sizes of 1024 x 280 pixels and 2560 x 600 pixels. You can get all the details by following this link. http://ct-social.com/twitter-header-template-2014/. You will also find a header template, and directions to help create an amazing header.

Getting Started

As I said earlier, tweets need to be short, sweet, and on target. You need to boil your message down to one quick point. That means you need to do a little planning before you start clicking the keys on your keyboard.

The first thing you need to do is select a tool to shorten the link you're going to use in your tweet. Two tools I recommend are **bitly** https://bitly.com/shorten/ and **Google URL Shortener** https://goo.gl/.

Here's an eBay URL for an Otterbox iPhone 6 case.

http://www.ebay.com/itm/NEW-Otterbox-Defender-Commuter-Symmetry-Case-for-Apple-iPhone-6-Plus-5-5-/321639090877?pt=LH_DefaultDomain_0&var=&hash=item4ae32f0abd

Here's the same link after it's been run through **bitly**.

http://ebay.to/1xZQSsC

Do you see the difference?

If you used the original link, it's 156 characters. That's more than you're allowed for your entire tweet. After bitly performs its magic, your link is down to a svelte 23 characters. That leaves plenty of characters to craft an amazing tweet.

Every tweet you send out needs to follow these three simple rules.

1. Boil your message down to just the essentials.
2. Use action words wherever possible.
3. Include a call to action.

An even better way to approach a promotional tweet would be to include a link to a short video on your blog, website, or YouTube. Let your followers watch the video first, then show them a link to your gig on Fiverr. It's less salesy and will focus more eyes on your tweet.

Here's another surprising factoid you need to consider. The shorter your tweet, the more likely people are to read it.

Research shows short tweets—between 80 to 100 characters are the most effective and tend to get read the most. That means the less you say; the more effective your tweet is going to be.

Lesson learned.

K. I. S. S.

Keep it simple stupid!

#Hashtags# - The Art of Getting Found

Getting found on Twitter revolves around using hashtags—better known as the # sign.

If you want to boil Twitter SEO down to the bare bones—this is it. Hashtags are nothing more than searchable keywords. When you use a hashtag, it makes it easier for other Twitter users to find your content.

Here are a few examples of hashtags currently used on Twitter.

- #CocaCola
- #MylieCyrus
- #ValentinesDay
- #WorldSeries
- #iPhone6
- #SuperBowlChampions

As you can see, hashtags are nothing more than keywords proceeded by the # sign. Sometimes users include more than one hashtag in a tweet: #Beatles #John #Paul #George #Ringo. You're not breaking any Twitter rules by using multiple hashtags, but I'd suggest keeping it to no more than two. Any more and readers are going to think you're screaming for attention, or suffering from a bad case of keyword spamming syndrome.

The first thing to remember is only use hashtags relevant to your business. Miley Cyrus is popular, and tweeting about her will get your tweet a lot of views, but it won't help your business.

Let's take my Fiverr business for example. At first glance, proofreading and copywriting services aren't very sexy, and they sure aren't at the top of Twitter's trending list. But, if I position them correctly—they are relevant to one small segment of the Twitterverse.

Try these tweets on for size, and pay extra attention to the hashtags.

- Need another eye on your #manuscript? We offer inexpensive #copywriting & #Proofreading services
- Unsure about the difference between a #comma and a #semicolon. #Proofreading changes everything
- Tired of bad book reviews? Professional #copyediting can keep the wolves at bay
- Not selling enough books. Your #book description makes the difference. Free critique.

Most of my posts follow the rule of one hashtag per tweet, but now and then I break the rule because my content appeals to several different market segments.

Another thing you will notice is most of my hashtags come in the center of the tweet, rather than at the beginning. It's counterintuitive to what you'd think, but recent research shows placing the hashtag in the center of the tweet is more effective. I'm not sure why, but it seems to work. Test it for yourself to see if it boosts your response rate.

Other businesses create a unique hashtag that includes their business name. It can be as simple as your name - #MoneyBagsPayDayLoans, or it can be a slogan - #BatteriesForLess. It may be a tag to help people discover your local business #QuadCityMagician or #DavenportDJ.

Whatever you decide for your hashtag strategy the key is to make it relevant. Choose hashtags that will help your business get discovered. If you're unsure whether a hashtag is a good fit for your business or not, run a search on Twitter and see what pops up.

Get Followed – Build Your Tribe

There's a lot of advice floating around about how to build your follower base. Some of it is good, some of it not so good. A lot of the *gurus* endorse the more is better syndrome. Paris Hilton has ten trillion followers, so you need to get that many, too.

That's not quite true.

Sean Platt, Johnny B. Truant, and David Wright put it best in their book, **Write. Publish. Repeat**. To be successful, you only need one thousand true fans. Their book is about building your career as an author, but the advice applies to any business trying to build a social media platform or fan base.

It doesn't take a bazillion followers to build your business. It just takes one thousand *true fans* who will buy every new product or service you release, then tell their friends about it.

Contrast this with the typical advice about how to grow your followers on Twitter.

Here's the way it goes.

Make a list of the big players in your field. Start following their followers. If after two days they don't follow you back, unfollow them. Rinse and repeat. Over time you will amass a large list of followers.

Don't get me wrong. It's an effective strategy, and it has worked well for many businesses that want to develop a massive number of followers. But, if you're a business, it's not about the number of followers you have, it's about the number of followers who will become customers and take action on your tweets.

Don't work harder than necessary.

Post eight to ten solid tweets a week. Offer valuable content your followers will enjoy and use. Keep the amount of self-promotion to a minimum. For every ten tweets you shoot out, no more than one or two should be salesy. If your followers get even the slightest hint you're more interested in selling to them than sharing with them they're going to unfollow you.

The key to success on Twitter is to provide great content that encourages readers to check out your bio and contact links. If you continue to provide pertinent content, the sales will follow.

I know this has been said before, but social media marketing is more of a marathon than a sprint. Short bursts will get you attention, but staying in the game over the long haul is how you win.

LinkedIn

LinkedIn is the world's largest network of professional and business users. It has over 250 million register users worldwide with a targeted income of over $100,000 per year. They are college educated, and tend to be older than users on other social networks—the average age is between 50 and 65. Sixty percent of LinkedIn users are located outside of the United States, so you're going to be working with a large international audience.

How important LinkedIn is as a social network for your Fiverr business is directly related to the services you offer.

If you're a service-oriented business offering resume writing, cover letters, and job coaching tips LinkedIn would be a perfect match for your target audience. If you approach it, right LinkedIn could be a great audience for sellers offering personalized videos, reminder, and virtual assistant services.

If you sell entertainment-related gigs, the value of LinkedIn is debatable. I would use LinkedIn to build connections with other Fiverr sellers and industry experts. This way you can share tips with vendors who offer similar services, explore new gig ideas, and learn about trending developments in your industry.

If you sell job coaching, resume, or interview services, I would work on building contacts, join career search groups, and continue to position myself as an expert job search coach. Post pictures, videos, and articles that position you as an expert in your industry. Join like-minded groups, answer questions in forums and communities, and work on optimizing your profile so people can find you.

Whatever you do—don't sell.

LinkedIn is a community of professionals. Other members will tune you out at the slightest indication you're trying to make a sale. Instead concentrate on sharing top quality information people will use, like, and appreciate. If you do this on a consistent basis, the right people will find you.

LinkedIn 101

The trick to being found on LinkedIn is to fill out your profile as completely as possible.

Before you do that, you need to determine what you want to accomplish. Do you want to get leads for the services you sell? Do you want to connect with leaders in your industry? Or do you just want to sell as many gigs as possible?

There are no wrong answers.

Just understand your goals determine how you should approach LinkedIn.

The first thing you need to do is create a well-optimized profile. It all starts with a professional photograph. Dress appropriately to your customer base. For men, if you're courting businessman, wear a suit. Otherwise, dress similar to the people you're trying to attract. For women, you can never go wrong with a dress or pantsuit. Tone the makeup down, and steer clear of flashy colors.

Next on the list is your headline. You've got 120 characters to make it work, so get down to brass tacks.

To get your headline right, you've got to think like the people you want to attract. What keywords are they likely to use to find you? Is your location important? Should you include some of the key services you offer? This is important because LinkedIn is going to use these keywords to display your profile in search. If you use the wrong keywords, you're going to be off the radar for over 90 percent of LinkedIn users.

LinkedIn has a new feature open to all users—a cover photo. It gives you one more chance to wow people who view your profile. Make sure it conveys your story. If you're an author, your cover photo should show the covers of your most relevant books. If you're selling something, it should show your key products being used by real people. If services are your game—list the services you offer in large letters. Show the benefits in a series of bullet points. If possible include a tagline, "Cover letters geared towards Fortune 500 executives." "Gourmet recipes so good they're sinfully delicious."

The optimal size for your cover photo is 1400 x 425 pixels. And, here's one more tip. Don't make your cover photo; hire a professional designer on Fiverr or Elance. It's too important to leave to chance.

If you get these three things right, you're ahead of ninety percent of the users on LinkedIn. Remember—Profile photo, headline, and cover photo.

Next up is your summary.

Tell your story. You've got 2,000 characters to tell visitors what you're all about, why they should deal with you, and why you're the right guy to solve their problem.

I'm an e-commerce writer, so I lead with my value statement. "Short easy to read solutions for your e-commerce problems." That sets the tone for everything else. It's a promise I make to readers and everything I say from this point on needs to make good on that promise and reinforce it.

Your summary should tell people about you. It's your value statement.

Brag a little bit.

Use this space to breathe a little life into your profile. Talk about what drives you. Your passions, your favorite sports teams, or a local charity you're active in. Or if you're all business: talk about your business. How'd you get into this line of work? What do you like about it? What value do you bring to the table for new customers?

After your summary comes work experience.

This is your traditional resume. For online sellers, this may or may not be relevant. If your past work experiences are relevant, include them. If it's not relevant or you prefer not to share your employment history, leave this section blank. Just add your online business.

If you want to shine, collect recommendations and endorsements from your customers. If you can get five to ten recommendations, it's going to make you stand out head-and-shoulders above your competition. No one else on Fiverr is doing this.

Another section highlights your volunteer experience. I'd recommend everyone take some time to fill this out. Volunteer experience is an excellent way to connect with like-minded individuals. It's going to humanize you in a way work experience won't. Let's go back to the example of our resume and cover letter writer. If he talks up his experience coaching clients at local homeless shelters, he's going to humanize himself in eyes of LinkedIn viewers. Most of them are going to think he's someone who cares about his community and the people in it. It's not going to bring tears to every reader's eyes, but I guarantee you—it's going to convince many LinkedIn users you're the guy.

Publications and Projects give you two additional ways to position yourself as an expert in your field. Highlight any books you contributed to, even if it's just a Xeroxed booklet you hand out to clients. It shows you know your stuff, and people value your experience. Projects are a way to highlight your organizational and management skills. The key to describing any projects or publications you've participated in is to slant them towards your online business.

How to Use LinkedIn

LinkedIn recently started letting users post content to the site—pictures, videos, and written content. It's an awesome opportunity to stand out and grow your authority.

My suggestion is to make short written posts of 350 to 750 words once or twice a week. If you can do it, post a 1500 to 2500-word article once a month. The easiest way to do this is to just start writing. Don't worry that you're not a writer. What you say doesn't have to be fancy. Often the best content is special, just because it contains the information people want and need.

If you're at a loss for ideas, think about trending topics in your niche, new products that are about to be released, and the everyday questions buyers ask you. Answer one or two questions in every post, and stick with it. Over time readers will come back week after week to find out what's next.

Success won't happen overnight. But if you're in it for the long haul, and post consistently you will build a following, and many of your readers will eventually check out the links to your Fiverr gigs.

Every so often you should shake things up.

Post a relevant photo or video. Include a short description that tells viewers why it's important. Curiosity will entice people to look.

Keep in mind, when you first get started the only ones who can see your posts are your contacts. As time goes by and they share your content with their followers, your network will grow, and more people will be aware of what you're doing.

Another way to connect with people on LinkedIn is to join groups.

Groups are simply congregations of like-minded individuals who post questions and discussions in a private area on LinkedIn. Members are free to comment and join in the conversation. One thing I'd suggest is to spend a few days checking out different groups and learning how the members interact. Whatever you do, don't just jump in and start commenting before you understand the dynamics of the group.

More than any other social media network LinkedIn is going to require you to be in it for the long haul. If you stick with it and keep interacting with other members, you will grow a strong network that will help to increase your sales.

About the Author

My books offer short easy to read solutions to your e-commerce problems. You can read most of my books in under an hour. The information can be used to help you sell more products on eBay and Amazon, services on Fiverr, or eBooks on Amazon and Kindle.

Selling online isn't a mystery. It doesn't even have to be difficult.

It's all about getting started. Many people I've talked with have this crazy fear of putting things up for sale on eBay and Amazon. Somehow, they get the idea they need to do this or that. They worry they don't know enough about what they're doing to do it right. They wonder what they should sell, and about whether they can even do it or not.

That's where my books come in.

They take you hand in hand and walk you through getting started selling on eBay, Amazon, and Fiverr. They show you how to market your Kindle book.

My goal is to help you over the speed bumps so that you can be more successful from the get-go.

What are you waiting for?

Most of my books are available as audiobooks, so if you prefer to listen rather than read, be sure to check them out.

March 1st, 2017

Nick Vulich
Davenport, Iowa

www.ingramcontent.com/pod-product-compliance
Lightning Source LLC
Chambersburg PA
CBHW020928180526
45163CB00007B/2933

* 9 7 8 1 5 4 8 3 9 3 1 7 5 *